MIGUEL CABRERA
Baseball Superstar

BY MATT DOEDEN

CAPSTONE PRESS
a capstone imprint

Sports Illustrated Kids Superstar Athletes are published by Capstone Press,
1710 Roe Crest Drive, North Mankato, Minnesota 56003.
www.capstonepub.com

Library of Congress Cataloging-in-Publication Data
Doeden, Matt.
  Miguel Cabrera : baseball superstar / by Matt Doeden.
    pages cm.—(Sports illustrated kids. Superstar athletes.)
  Includes bibliographical references and index.
  Summary: "Introduces readers to the life of pro baseball star Miguel Cabrera"—Provided by publisher.

ISBN 978-1-4765-8602-1 (library binding)
ISBN 978-1-4765-9431-6 (paperback)
1. Cabrera, Miguel, 1983– —Juvenile literature. 2. Baseball players—Venezuela—Biography—Juvenile literature.
3. Baseball players—United States—Biography—Juvenile literature. I. Title.
GV865.C25D64 2014
796.357092—dc23
  [B]   2013034375

Editorial Credits
Nate LeBoutillier, editor; Lori Bye, designer; Eric Gohl, media research; Eric Manske, production specialist

Photo Credits
AP Photo: Alan Diaz, 6, Four Seam Images/Mike Janes, 10; Newscom: Ai Wire Photo Service/Mike Jula, 12,
Reuters/STR, 5; Shutterstock: Photo Works, 22 (top); Sports Illustrated: Al Tielemans, 1, 21, 23, David E. Klutho,
2–3, 22 (bottom), John Biever, 15, 16, 19, Robert Beck, cover (all), 22 (middle), Simon Bruty, 24, Walter Iooss Jr., 9

Design Elements
Shutterstock/chudo-yudo, designerpix, Fassver Anna, Fazakas Mihaly

Direct Quotations
Page 7, from June 20, 2003, *ESPN* article "Cabrera's First Homer Gives Marlins Dramatic Win" www.espn.com
Page 18 and 20, from October 4, 2012, *ESPN* article "Miguel Cabrera Wins Triple Crown" www.espn.com

Printed in the United States of America in North Mankato, Minnesota.

092013   007771CGS14

TABLE OF CONTENTS

CHAPTER 1

WELCOME TO THE BIG LEAGUES

Miguel Cabrera was having a rough day. In his first at bat, the Florida Marlins leftfielder had struck out. In the ninth inning, he grounded out, blowing a chance to win the game. Just 20 years old, Cabrera was playing his first big league game.

walk-off home run—a home run that ends the game, giving the home team a victory

The game went into extra innings. The Marlins and Tampa Bay Devil Rays were tied 1-1 in the 11th inning. Cabrera stepped to the plate. The Tampa Bay pitcher wound up and threw. Cabrera swung. Crack! The ball sailed 419 feet (127 meters) over the centerfield fence. Home run! The Marlins rushed onto the field to celebrate. Cabrera was just the third player in big league history to hit a **walk-off home run** in his first game.

"My first day in the big leagues, my first hit's a home run. It's good."
— Miguel Cabrera

CHAPTER 2

BORN INTO BASEBALL

Jose Miguel Torres Cabrera was born April 18, 1983, in Maracay, Venezuela. His father had been a good baseball player. His mother was a star on Venezuela's national softball team. Cabrera spent hours practicing on the field next to his house.

BASEBALL IDOL

Cabrera grew up idolizing big league shortstop Dave Concepcion. The Cincinnati Reds legend was also from Maracay. Concepcion played 19 seasons in the big leagues and made 9 All-Star teams.

Dave Concepcion

Cabrera was a natural ballplayer. By the time he was a teenager, major league **scouts** were watching him play. Many teams wanted to sign him. Cabrera chose to sign with his favorite team, the Marlins. At age 17 he began his baseball career in the minor leagues. He started out as a shortstop. He later switched to third base and outfield.

scout—a person whose job is to watch and evaluate players

Cabrera's career started slowly. In 2000 he hit just two home runs in 65 games during his first minor league season. He worked to improve. By 2003 Cabrera was having a great season for the Carolina Mudcats. He was called up to the big leagues in June. Cabrera went on to help the Marlins win the 2003 World Series. In Game 4 against the New York Yankees, Cabrera hit a memorable home run off of pitching legend Roger Clemens.

CHAPTER 3

BIG LEAGUE STAR

Cabrera spent his first five seasons with the Marlins. He was a complete hitter. He always had a high batting average. He also hit a lot of home runs. Cabrera was named to the National League All-Star team every season from 2004 to 2007.

The Marlins traded Cabrera to the Detroit Tigers after the 2007 season. Cabrera led the American League with 37 home runs in 2008. In 2011 he hit .344 to win the American League batting title. He also hit four home runs in the playoffs. The Tigers were just two wins away from going to the World Series but lost to the Texas Rangers.

NUMBER 300

In 2012 Cabrera hit his 300th career home run. He joined his countryman Andrés Galarraga as the only Venezuelan-born players to reach that milestone. Galarraga hit 399 homers in 19 big league seasons.

Cabrera had an amazing 2012 season. He became the first hitter since 1967 to win the **triple crown**. He led the American League in batting average (.330), home runs (44), and **RBIs** (139). He led the Tigers to the World Series, but they lost to the San Francisco Giants. In 2013 Cabrera won the American League batting title for a third straight season. The Tigers won the Central Division but fell short of the World Series.

triple crown—an achievement in baseball in which a hitter leads his league in batting average, home runs, and runs batted in
RBI—stands for run batted in

CHAPTER 4

SLUGGING SUPERSTAR

Cabrera has come a long way since playing as a teen in Venezuela. He rose quickly to the big leagues and became an instant star. His rare ability to hit for power and average has made him one of baseball's most dangerous hitters.

"He's the best hitter in the game. You leave one pitch over the plate that at-bat, and he's going to hit it."
— Angels outfielder Mike Trout, on Cabrera

TIMELINE

1983—Miguel Cabrera is born on April 18 in Maracay, Venezuela.

1999—Cabrera signs a contract with the Florida Marlins.

2003—Cabrera hits a walk-off home run in his first major league game; the Marlins win the World Series.

2007—Cabrera is traded to the Detroit Tigers.

2008—Cabrera leads the American League with 37 home runs in his first season as a Tiger.

2011—Cabrera wins the American League batting title.

2012—Cabrera wins the triple crown, is named American League MVP, and leads the Tigers to the World Series.

2013—Cabrera wins the American League batting title and leads the Tigers to the Central Division crown.

GLOSSARY

RBI (RBI)—stands for run batted in

scout (SKOWT)—a person whose job is to watch and evaluate players

triple crown (TRIP-uhl CROWN)—an achievement in baseball in which a player leads his league in batting average, home runs, and runs batted in

walk-off home run (WALK-OFF HOME RUN)—a home run that ends the game, giving the home team a victory

READ MORE

Doeden, Matt. *The World's Greatest Baseball Stars.* Sports Illustrated Kids. Mankato, Minn.: Capstone Press, 2010.

Fishman, Jon M. *Miguel Cabrera.* Minneapolis: Lerner Publications Company, 2013.

Stewart, Mark. *The Detroit Tigers.* Chicago: Norwood House Press, 2012.

INTERNET SITES

FactHound offers a safe, fun way to find Internet sites related to this book. All of the sites on FactHound have been researched by our staff.

Here's all you do:
Visit *www.facthound.com*
Type in this code: 9781476586021

 Check out projects, games and lots more at
www.capstonekids.com

INDEX